baby einstein®

Shapes

The Walt Disney Company

Hyperion Books for Children, New York

For information address Hyperion Books for Children, 114 Fifth Avenue, New York, New York 10011-5690.
Printed in China
Library of Congress Cataloging Card Number on file.
ISBN 0-7868-3804-3

Great Minds Start Little.™

If you're looking for a circle, you might just find a 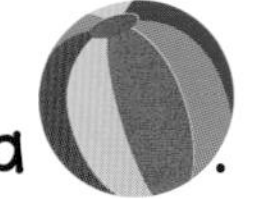.

Or you might spy a round  hanging on the wall.

A 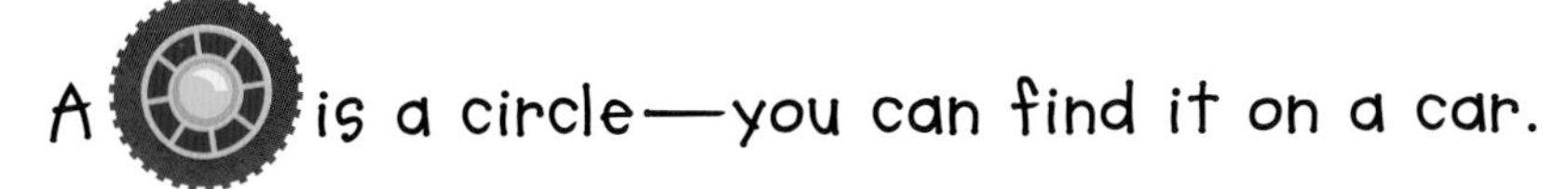 is a circle—you can find it on a car.

To find circles in your house,

you don't need to look far.

Triangles have three straight sides. Did you know that?

Just like an ice cream  or  on a cat.

My  flag is a triangle; its sails are triangles, too.

Can you think of triangle shapes? It's not so hard to do.

In my playroom there are many squares.

Like  I stack with careful flair. My  is a silly square.

And square 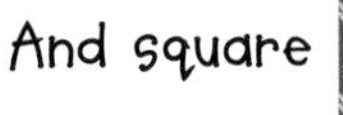 are stacked up in the air.

In our kitchen there are so many ovals to find—

Like the that Mom cooks at breakfast time! A is

a yummy oval treat. For dessert, it's that I love to eat!

Without four-sided rectangles, what would we do?

A house would be quite dark without a to look through.

We wouldn't have our kitchen , we wouldn't have a ,

We wouldn't have a bedroom for our bedroom floor.

Did you know that diamonds can be lots of fun?

Think of 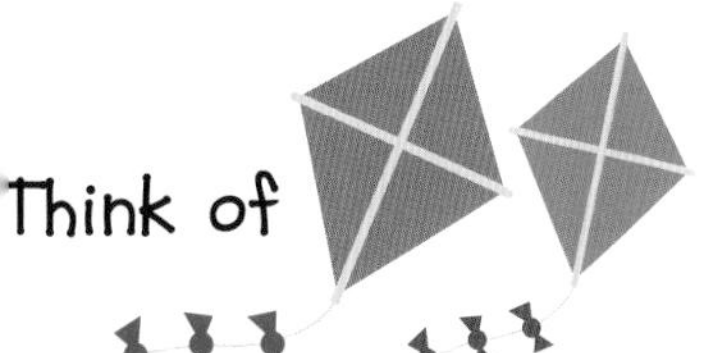 flying in the summer sun.

We play baseball on a 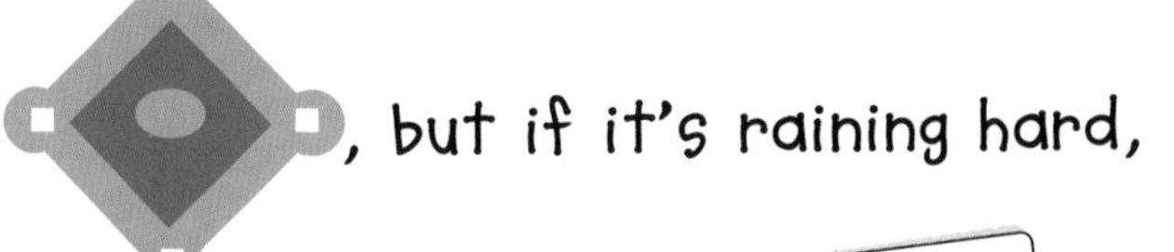, but if it's raining hard,

Then we go inside to play with diamonds on our !

A circle is a crazy thing,

It has no sides, just one round ring.

You’ll see a circle on my nose—

Now find five more beneath my toes.

The horns upon my head are gold

And shaped like triangles, I am told.

A triangle has three straight sides.

Can you find three more, besides?

My tower of blocks is very tall,

And made of squares, both big and small.

Each square has four sides, all the same—

Find all the squares to play this game.

The oval shapes that fill my nest

Are eggs that need a lot of rest.

Now, note their oval shape with care,

Then look for ovals in the air.

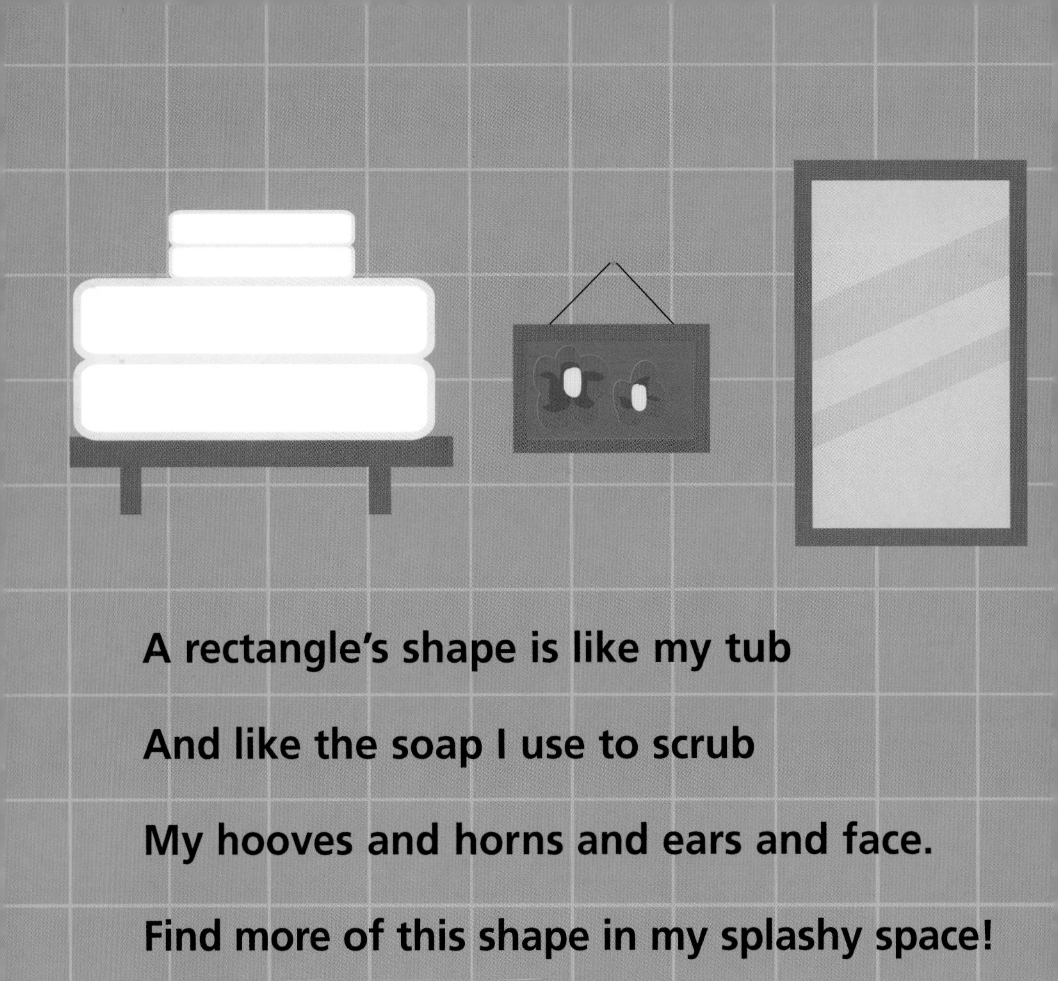

A rectangle's shape is like my tub

And like the soap I use to scrub

My hooves and horns and ears and face.

Find more of this shape in my splashy space!

SOAP

Have you seen my diamond kite?

It's green and orange and blue and white.

The wind has blown it all about,

Find four more diamonds, point them out.

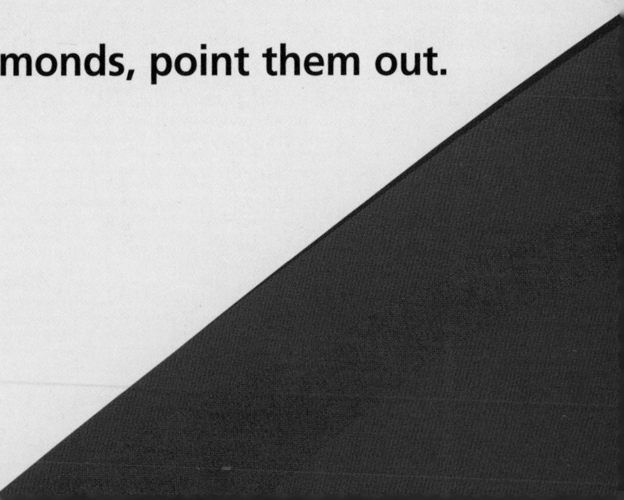